Travel to work

WITHDRAWN

mail delivery

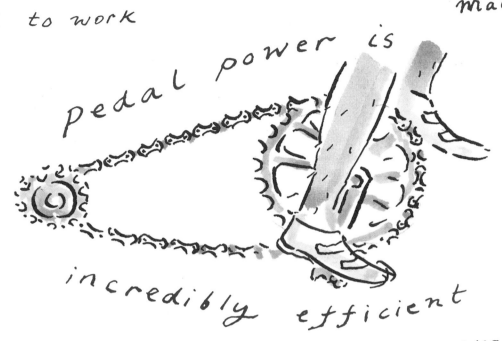

pedal power is

incredibly efficient

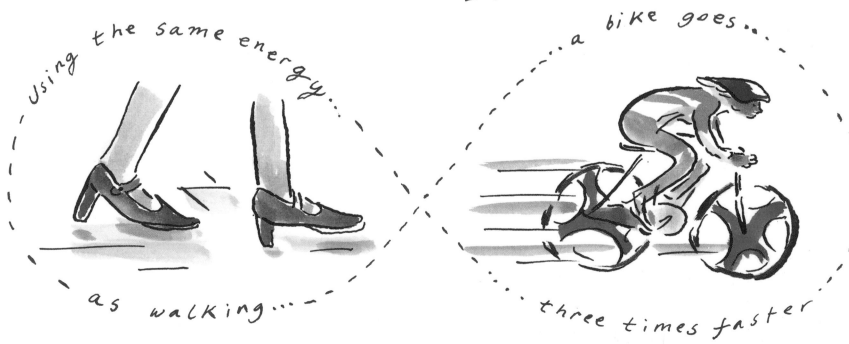

Using the same energy...

...a bike goes...

...as walking...

...three times faster

Fifty years ago, very few cyclists had helmets.

Today is different. Be safe, wear a helmet!
—A.D.

tandem bike

For George,
with love from Dad

Farrar Straus Giroux Books for Young Readers
An imprint of Macmillan Publishing Group, LLC
175 Fifth Avenue, New York 10010

Copyright © 2017 by Allan Drummond
Color separations by Bright Arts (H. K.) Ltd.
Printed in China by Toppan Leefung Printing Ltd.,
Dongguan City, Guangdong Province
Designed by Kristie Radwilowicz
First edition, 2017
1 3 5 7 9 10 8 6 4 2

mackids.com

Library of Congress Cataloging-in-Publication Data

Names: Drummond, Allan, author.
Title: Pedal power : how one community became the bicycle capital of the
    world / Allan Drummond.
Description: First edition. | New York : Farrar Straus Giroux Books for Young
    Readers, 2017 | Audience: Age 4–8.
Identifiers: LCCN 2016028791 | ISBN 9780374305277 (hardcover)
Subjects: LCSH: Bicycles—Netherlands—Amsterdam—Safety measures—Juvenile
    literature. | City planning—Netherlands—Amsterdam—Juvenile literature.
Classification: LCC HE5739.N4 D78 2016 | DDC 388.3/47209492352—dc23
LC record available at https://lccn.loc.gov/2016028791

Our books may be purchased in bulk for promotional, educational, or business use. Please
contact your local bookseller or the Macmillan Corporate and Premium Sales Department at
(800) 221-7945 ext. 5442 or by e-mail at MacmillanSpecialMarkets@macmillan.com.

training wheels

FSC
www.fsc.org
MIX
Paper from
responsible sources
FSC® C104723

chopper bike

cargo bike

allan drummond

pedal

power

How One Community Became the Bicycle Capital of the World

Farrar Straus Giroux
New York

Today, if you visit the city of Amsterdam in the Netherlands, you'll see people on bicycles buzzing about everywhere:

over canal bridges,

down narrow streets,

across busy roads.

Ding! Ding! Ding!

To school,

to work,

to shop,

to visit friends.

All kinds of bikes.

Thousands of bikes—
more bikes than cars!

Ding! Ding!

Amsterdam is known worldwide as the capital city of cycling. Cars and trucks are allowed on the streets, but they have to drive carefully. Bikes rule the road.

After you!

Ding! Ding!

Now *that's* pedal power.

But it wasn't always like this. In the 1970s, Amsterdam, like most big cities, had a lot of vehicle traffic, and the roads were starting to become too dangerous for cyclists.

So how did Amsterdam become the bike capital of the world?
Well, it took some very special people to make that change. Young
moms like Maartje Rutten and her friends—and their children.

Every day Maartje and her son saw fine old buildings being destroyed to make way for gigantic highways.

Extra-wide streets and long, dark tunnels were built for all the new vehicle traffic, but there was no space for bicycles.

Crossing the huge, busy roads by bicycle became almost impossible.

Ding! Ding!

Screech! Crunch!

Taking a bike to school or work or to visit friends was a dangerous thing to do.

"Something's wrong," said Maartje. "The roads belong to all of us, not just cars and trucks."

Her friends agreed. "Cities like Amsterdam need bikes."

KOFFIEHUIS

Everyone began to speak up.

Word got around and people started protesting, not just in Amsterdam but all over the Netherlands.

At first the demonstrations were great fun. People even held parties in the middle of the road.
"Give us back our streets!" they cried.

Beep!

Beep!

Beep!

Crowds gathered outside the Dutch prime minister's house.
They chanted songs and called for change.

Children banded together and proclaimed that some roads
should be closed to make play-streets.

Television and newspaper
reporters loved all the stories. The
protests seemed like great fun.

Then one terrible day, a different story appeared in the news. A young girl cycling to school had been killed by a car.

The child's father, Vic Langenhoff, was a newspaper reporter, and he wrote something that hardly anyone could believe.

"This year, five hundred children have been killed on the roads of our country. Many of them were riding bikes."

It was true. The situation was deadly serious. Something had to be done.

Now everyone was angry. The marches got noisier.
More and more people came out onto the streets to demand safe places to walk and cycle.

Meanwhile, drivers were angry, too. The country was running out of fuel, and the government announced a new regulation: "No cars in Amsterdam on Sunday."

And that gave Maartje an incredible idea.

"We'll cycle through the big new tunnel. We'll show them!" she said.
"But it's against the law. The tunnel is only for cars!" her friends cried.
"That's exactly the problem," said Maartje. "We need to take back the roads."

The streets of Amsterdam were silent when Maartje, her friends, and their children gathered at the mouth of the tunnel.

"We can't!" someone said.

"Who knows what will happen to us?"

But Maartje was determined. "Let's do it! Today's the day!" she shouted.

And they all set off into the darkness.

The sound of bicycle bells echoed off the tunnel walls.

Down, down, and along they went.

Ding! Ding! Ding!

Pedal power!

Bikes not cars

As they rode toward the brightness at the other end, they saw policemen and flashing lights waiting ahead.

"It's the cops!" someone shouted. "Let's turn back!"

"Keep going!" said Maartje. She stood up on her pedals and pushed on.

The police had blocked the road.
"This is a cars-only tunnel," they said. "You cyclists have broken the law."

The officers lifted up the children and their little bikes and put them into police cars.

"It's just not safe," they said.

Back at the police station, everyone was served lemonade and cookies. *That's strange,* thought Maartje. And she noticed that the policemen were smiling just a little bit. *That wasn't so bad. Maybe all of this protesting is working,* she thought.

And she was quite right. That day was just the beginning.
Maartje and her friends came up with lots of good ideas to allow bikes,
people, and cars to all share the streets peacefully.

They proposed special bike lanes on busy routes,

traffic bumps and curves in the roads to slow down vehicles,

and new laws giving bikes the right-of-way over cars.

And, finally,
people listened!

Amsterdam led the way, and that's why it's the bike capital of the world.

Today, we see these ideas at work all over, from Tokyo

to New York City

and all over China.

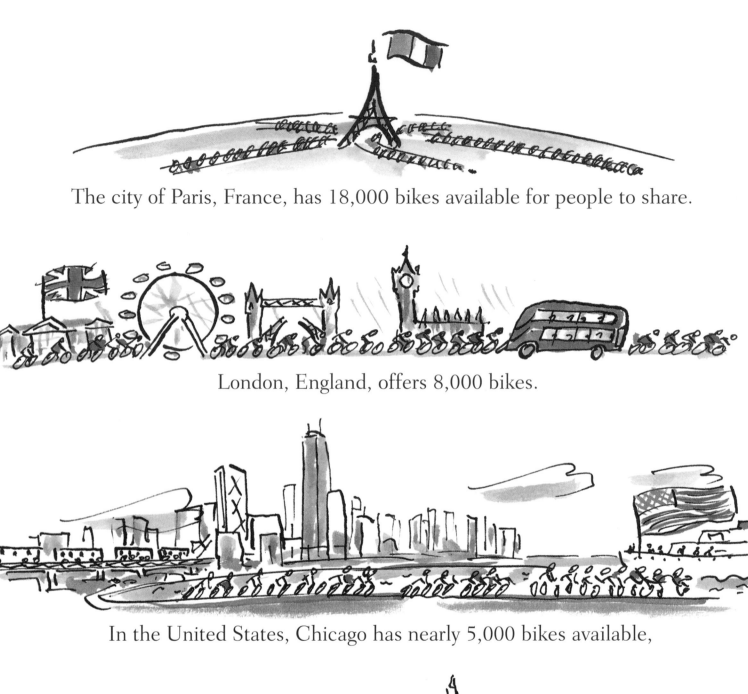

The city of Paris, France, has 18,000 bikes available for people to share.

London, England, offers 8,000 bikes.

In the United States, Chicago has nearly 5,000 bikes available,

and Shanghai, China, offers 50,000 for visitors and residents to ride.

And cycling keeps you fit.

A bike is quiet.

It takes up less road space,

and, of course, it doesn't pollute the air.

A bike doesn't need
fuel—our legs do it all!

And what happened to Maartje Rutten?
Well, today her name is Maartje van Putten,

and you can still see her whizzing around
the streets of Amsterdam on her bike.
Now *that's* pedal power!

AUTHOR'S NOTE

When I started working on this book, I wanted to write and illustrate about how wonderful it feels to ride a bike, particularly in a city. I also wanted to show how amazingly energy-efficient bicycles are. Quite soon the words *pedal power* popped into my head, and I knew that this would be the title.

On my journey of discovery, I looked at the history of bikes and learned about all the crazy shapes that people tried before the design we know today. I also read about the incredible trips people made on two wheels. When I came across the story of Maartje Rutten and the Amsterdam protests, I realized that the words *pedal power* meant so much more.

So I went to Amsterdam to meet Maartje and see for myself. She showed me her lovely big bike, and one of the first things she said was "Cities need bikes." That simple statement is at the heart of this book. Bikes, said Maartje, have the power to make city life better.

I thought about how when I was young my bike took me on adventures that I still remember today. When I was an art student in London, I used my bike every day. I was fearless and enjoyed taking on the traffic. The first time I battled with the red buses and black taxis passing Buckingham Palace, I felt as if I were king of the road. It was great fun—but dangerous. You had to be young, brave, and fit to even attempt cycling in London.

Since those days, just like in Maartje's Amsterdam, the number of vehicles in all our cities has continued to grow. Only a few years ago, it seemed as if motor traffic had won the battle.

But today London, like Amsterdam, is much more cycle-friendly. Every week sees another stretch of precious street painted blue and made into a bike lane. Motorists now have to pay to enter the city's center on workdays. All of this is making life a little better and, in my opinion, much fairer for everyone.

It looks as if the whole world is now following in the tracks of pioneers like Maartje. Hopefully soon, riding a bike in London or any other city will not be just for the young, brave, and fit. Anyone should be able to jump on a bike and buzz about safely, secure in knowing that they truly have pedal power. *Ding! Ding!*

BIBLIOGRAPHY

For more information, check out these sources:

"How Child Road Deaths Changed the Netherlands." Radio story, *Witness*, BBC World Service, November 27, 2013. bbc.co.uk/programmes/p01lw88k

"How the Dutch Got Their Cycle Paths." YouTube video, BicycleDutch, October 9, 2011. youtube.com/watch?v=XuBdf9jYj7o

"Lessons from the Netherlands: Report from the London Cycling Campaign Study Tour of Three Dutch Cities." London Cycling Campaign, October 2011. cycling-embassy.org.uk/sites/cycling-embassy.org.uk/files/documents/Lessons+from+the+Netherlands+1-1.5+FULL+SIZE.pdf

"Stop de Kindermoord." BicycleDutch. bicycledutch.wordpress.com/tag/stop-de-kindermoord (retrieved 3/18/2016).

"Stop the Child Murder." A View from the Cycle Path. aviewfromthecyclepath.com/2011/01/stop-child-murder.html (retrieved 3/18/2016).

Great Cyclists

Thomas Stevens
around the world 1884–1886

Annie Kopchovsky
around the world 1894–1895

Sir Bradley Wiggins

Charles Minthorn Murphy
one mile in a minute 1899

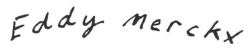

Eddy Merckx
HOLTEN
hour record 1972